HISTORY

David O'Hanlon was born in Portsmouth in 1987, and is now based in Northumberland. His poems have appeared in *The Rialto*, *And Other Poems*, *Acumen* and *Dream Catcher*, amongst others. His debut pamphlet *art brut* was published by V. Press in 2015.

# History

### David O'Hanlon

*Valley Press*

First published in 2016 by Valley Press
Woodend, The Crescent, Scarborough, YO11 2PW
www.valleypressuk.com

ISBN 978-1-908853-57-8
Cat. no. VP0078

Copyright © David O'Hanlon 2016

The right of David O'Hanlon to be identified as the
author of this work has been asserted in accordance with
the Copyright, Designs and Patents Act 1988.

All rights reserved. No part of this publication may be
reproduced, stored in or introduced into a retrieval system,
or transmitted in any form, by any means (electronic,
mechanical, photocopying, recording or otherwise) without
prior written permission from the rights holders.

A CIP record for this book is available from the British Library.

www.valleypressuk.com/authors/davidohanlon

# Contents

*A Philosophical Enquiry into the Origin of
Our Ideas of the Sublime and Beautiful*  9
Fall  10
Pyramus and Thisbe  11
Narcissus  12
Pygmalion  13
Proteus  15
Danaus  16
Orpheus  17
Tantalus  18
Tereus  19
The Fall  20
Sisyphus  21
Cassandra  22
A toymaker of some renown  23
Alcibiades  24
The Line  28
Poem in Which the Sky Doesn't Crack  30
Rabbit  31
Yo-yo  32
Cusp  34
Eurydice  35
Icons  36
Bildungsroman  37
Reality  43
As It Was  44
History  45

'God cannot alter the past, historians can'

SAMUEL BUTLER

*A Philosophical Enquiry into the Origin of
Our Ideas of the Sublime and Beautiful*

This book has only
been checked out –
if the stamps
and not the look of it

are to be believed –
seven times in its history.
The last (before me)
was thirteen years ago,

the first in 1959,
a month before –
would you believe it

to look at me? –
I was born.
I'm on Section Three.

# Fall

*in memory of George Mills*

I

I came out that night as a goth:
leather, chains, black nails.
It was Friday fish and chips with the family.
My granddad stood to tell the table

(parents, brothers, aunt, uncle):
*There are two types
of people who paint their nails: women
and woofters.*

II

Last time I saw him he remembered
who I was, though he didn't look
at me directly. He watched me in the mirror:
saw me as I see myself.

But how did I see him? In a chair
he couldn't raise himself from,
bruised from a fall two nights before,
his fingers black.

# Pyramus and Thisbe

She sits on a chair tucked between
the oven and the worktop.
A book of wordsearches
lies open on her lap.

Poirot – on the TV squeezed
between the freezer
and ceiling – in a way
too different from the novel

solves another murder,
while the mug of sherry
at her elbow
solves everything else.

The other side of a wall,
he switches channels
every few minutes –
*Murder, She Wrote* to *Sharpe*,

*Dad's Army* back to *Murder, She Wrote* –
not looking for a story.
The cup of tea she made him
goes cold in his hand.

# Narcissus

*after Ovid*

Narcissus, in his old age, used to tell
all those who came down to his river
how, like the story of the flower,
love at first sight is a myth.

*I knelt on the bank to drink*
*and was caught by beauty, for days saw*
*nothing more than a face*
*and its gently trembling features,*

*but what I grew to love*
*is how he looks at me, the silent joy*
*he finds in my laugh, the shock waves*
*sent through him as my tears hit the surface.*

*He takes my tales and doesn't question*
*the truth of Teiresias and Echo.*
*(Why run? She was my type.)*
*As I speak them over, he mouths the words.*

And here's the mark of true love:
they died the same day.

# Pygmalion

*after Ovid*

That night
she wasn't stone.
He ran his hands
over his work

and felt her warmth,
kissed her
and felt a tongue
he didn't carve.

Stone yielded
at his touch
like wax softened
by his fingers.

He was afraid
he'd bruise
the perfect white
of her skin

as he explored her,
discovered
unknown regions
and was lost.

She turned
her eyes to heaven
as he cried out
to the gods.

In the morning,
dust and grit lay
in the folds of his skin,
his whole body raw.

## Proteus

I was born to be a fisherman like my father
and then I changed

I was a soldier and I saw the dead
and then I changed

I got lost in the gothic cathedral of my self
and then I changed

I believed and I prayed for my soul
and then I changed

I was an abstract and abstracted painter
and then I changed

I was once in love
and then I changed

I am an old man who cannot hold his shape
and I am changing

# Danaus

When my daughter played outside,
she'd carry with her round the garden,
hugged to her chest, a cracked earthen vase,
dripping water. She wouldn't let me replace it

or fix the cracks. The drops marked out
a breadcrumb trail over the decking
and the paving slabs. Never would she
reveal to me the inner secret of her game.

I'd watch from the window,
and Lucretius would muddy my thoughts:
he said *if the body's a vessel,
then the water in it's the soul,*

and each drip was time and nature
taking its toll. The price we all pay.
But I shake such nonsense away.
It's just a vase and water and a game,

a game the joy of which, as she grew older,
drained away, and now her little earthen vase
stands empty by the door,
but tries to fill with water when it rains.

# Orpheus

Listen. Against the hush of midnight:
the scribble of pencil on paper.
Iambic pentameter:
this is how he'll raise the dead.

*da dum da dum da dum da dum da dum*

The heart of Death softens,
breaks. Eyes closed, he listens –
yes, those are her footsteps on the stairs,
yes, those are her footsteps in the hall,

*da dum da dum da dum da dum da dum*

yes, the door creaks at her push,
breaths so small they'd be inaudible
if he wasn't sure he felt them on his neck.
The rhythm of his pencil

*da dum da dum da dum da dum da dum*

stops. He looks over his shoulder
and she isn't there.
Against the hush of midnight:
the scribble of pencil on paper. Listen.

## Tantalus

*I know I'll never reach*
*the hanging fruit, know*
*the chest-high waters will recede*
*every time I bow to drink.*

*And so, for all eternity,*
*I'll stand here resolute.*
*I'll never strive for the out-of-reach*
*nor bend a knee for anyone*

*or anything.*
But his stomach clenches
like his fists. He,
and his resolution, break.

# Tereus

Your song, your lament,
convinces me to take my memories
and my grief outside.

And I'm glad: I might have
missed the sun catch its own
reflection in a puddle

and fall in love. Remind me,
little nightingale,
are you Procne or Philomel?

## The Fall

*'Falling and flying are near-identical sensations,
in all but one final detail'*
— *Don Paterson*

and as I turned to walk away
I knocked her ersatz Grecian urn

which fell like Sappho
from the cliffs of Leucadia
all for the love of Phaon

fell like Troy
for the love of Helen

fell like Icarus
for the love of flight

fell like Satan
for love of himself

fell like man
for the love of God

fell like I fell
and broke

# Sisyphus

And the boulder rolls back
down the hill. I almost laugh.
I've wept enough. This is my joy:
to see that globe, my entire world,

fall away and – ha! – crash,
then to descend in its wake,
relishing the downhill run,
arms thrown out, a child again.

# Cassandra

I'm circled by the stages of my life.
My two-year-old self holds hands with a doll,
and there's me at seven in calico and pigtails.
Teenage me hidden by too much make-up.
Look at me, jubilantly graduating.
Here I'm pregnant with my son.

And there's me as I am now,
mirroring my very move.

There I'm suited for the job I'll work
for decades. There retired.
There sat down, unable to stand.
Finally, there's my ghost,
the only me who doesn't look up,
for in her arms is my newborn self.

## A toymaker of some renown

sent his ex-wife the gift
of an exquisite
little horse: sorrel-flock,
a sable mane, a sable tail, a fetlock

raised. And inside he sealed
three plastic soldiers: crude,
immovable, unpainted,
shop-bought in their hundreds.

# Alcibiades

*after Plato*

'Great minds speak of ideas, average minds of events.
Small minds speak of people.' — *Socrates*

I

It drew a crowd, the statue of Socrates.
A Gordian knot had bound him there
from rosy-fingered dawn to dusk.
We could almost see his thoughts

circle him like a halo, his face upturned
as though awaiting birds to form
an omen in the air, and I knew: it's a puzzle,
not another's eyes, turns Socrates to stone.

We brought out blankets and pillows
and slept out in the cool to see
if he'd remain until the sun came up.
He did. Then went home without a word.

II

He reminds me of those statues of Silenus
you see in statuaries'. There's an uncanny resemblance,
don't you think? The beard, bald head, flat nose.
That superior curve of the lips. The round belly.

It's as though, in secret, he models for every sculptor
in the city; a vanity belied by his appearance.
(I mean, it's such a rarity to see him like this:
bathed, sandals on his feet).

And of course, those figures of the
drunken teacher are crafted hollow,
made to open and filled with tiny icons,
delicate sculptures of gods that tumble out.

III

His talk reminds me of Marsyas the satyr, the silenus
who taught Olympus the music of his namesake.

His flute and fingers shaped his breath to songs
which defined his listeners as the sum of all their faults,

melodies which, if mimicked by you or me on old reed pipes,
would still entrance the listener, reduce them to nothing.

So Socrates's tongue turns all he exhales to charms,
the language and learnings of a god,

and speaking of nothing: mules and roads,
smiths and cobblers, air and dirt.

IV

He's a siren. It's a song
with a simple promise:
you'll be a wiser man.
I have to clog my ears with wax

or crash against his rocks
and grow old
having never left his side,
my armies and offices abandoned.

V

Apart from him, I'm like a runaway slave.
Every sound is my slaver coming to reclaim me.
Who in these circumstances
wouldn't have my reputation?

I tremble at any word that resembles
his name and tell nightingales
I wish he'd vanish from the earth,
or at least turn to stone.

## The Line

The headphones sign
their name across the floor.
That murmur is them practicing
saying what I need to hear.

∞

A thread hangs off her sleeve;
a knotted, twisted
symbol at her side.
Its meaning isn't clear.

∞

If a ribbon in a small girl's hair
catches on her father's watch
the infinite will come undone.

∞

The line of people queued outside
(for entry, for escape)
is wound around the building.

∞

My name is in pieces. Has been for years.
Since I abandoned cursive, in fact.

∞

The outline of two hippos in love.
Don't colour it in.
Keep it black and white.

∞

The hollow statue of a clown
was knocked off the table.
A strip of tape
holds the fragments together.

∞

*This isn't the South, anymore,*
*we're in the North.*
*The border's long-passed.*
A line I didn't know I'd crossed.

∞

My great-grandmother at the curb
watching car on car flash past:
*if you want to be on the other side*
*you had to be born there.*

∞

To my baby boy:
*I pray that I am not my father,*
*you your father's son.*

## Poem in Which the Sky Doesn't Crack

I met her by the station
beneath breaking clouds.

She looked well
and she was sorry:

she didn't know
who else to call.

But I smiled, I spoke,
as people often do,

carried her bags to the car
and drove her home,

and the sky didn't crack
as the sky never does.

*The sky never cracks.*
I wrote this before.

# Rabbit

Playing on the hill where we always played
we found a rabbit who wouldn't run away.

His little eyes were drops of blood.
A man in the pub Sam lived above

was a vet. He spoke a curse
that none among us understood: *myxomatosis*.

He took it to the trees to break its neck
so we wouldn't see. Which we didn't.

# Yo-yo

His bright green yo-yo
rolled out of his hand
and hung spinning at his ankle,

spinning like the waltzer at the fair
in France he snuck me on
when I was too small to ride,

spinning like the Catherine wheel
which needed poking to get it going
and which blinded my uncle Jack,

spinning like *your grandad*
*must be spinning in his grave at the thought*
*of these fascists getting into power*,

spinning like the yarns
my grandmother spun
of Ireland and the church

and her own grandmother's sin
of being old, unable
to walk up the hill to get to mass,

spinning like the wheel
of the bike she lay by
as she lay there at the roadside,

spinning by some science
I still don't understand,
until he reined it in
with a flick of his hand.

# Cusp

It was taken by James that first summer.
The angle's pretty low
but you can still see the river,
that thin dark crack through the background.
We're both sat cross-legged:
I'm knotting grass, you're saluting the sun.
Our knees almost touch
like God's hand and Adam's…

I use it as a bookmark (for now
it marks my whereabouts in Fournier's
*Lost Estate*) because with each look,
each dose of it, my tolerance increases.
It has a few nicks, a few folds.
It's about to begin to fade.

# Eurydice

*after Weldon Kees*

She seats us on the sofa in the place
where we must always sit. Tonight,
we watch *Toy Story*, and I smile
as they blur the boundary separating

falling from flight. She giggles
and describes exactly what she's watched
as though she hasn't seen it
a hundred times before.

And her commentary remains
while my eyes are on the screen,
just as only when these toys aren't watched
will they remain alive,

but when I look over
to the spot where she should sit,
there I see no daughter
but the spectre of a space

and that corner of the cemetery
where toys tend the graves.

# Icons

*in memory of Greta Hand*

I pray that there's an afterlife. You prayed
because you knew there was. At least,
the icons, the crosses, the ivory last supper,
the ersatz-prayer by that great poet,
Anonymous, pinned to your toilet door,
convinced me to believe that you believed;
though you never once spoke of God.
I pray you're looking down on us
like Jesus looks down from your wall.
I pray that there are clouds
and wings and haloes like the painting
by your bookcase packed with Poirots
and Miss Marples. I pray that there are angels.
I pray my truth contains no truth:
void, silence, a shroud of black
beneath which you can't know, have or be;
can't analyse the life you've shed;
can't hear this poem being read.
I pray for you, but more for me. I pray.

# Bildungsroman

*Skies*

*The sky touches the ground.*
That's what Mrs Lewis
used to tell me
when I drew that

blue ribbon across
the tops of pictures.
She also said
the sky's the limit.


*Columbus*

Men falling off
the edge of the earth
in the medieval tableaux
of a six-year-old.

Columbus alone thought
the world wasn't flat.
Or so they say.
It isn't true.

*Willow*

Under the unkempt hair
of the weeping willow
like a thought inside its head

Mrs Newman read to us from
*The Firework-Maker's Daughter*,
a tale whose end I still don't know.


*Shakespeare*

The projector threw Shakespeare
up against the wall. We,
in learning-position

(you guessed it: cross-legged)
clapped out his iambic pentameter,
applauded his death.

*Gods*

A plastic fir. My own image
distorted in a bauble.

It's hypocritical (*what did that
mean?*) to believe in Santa

and not Jesus. But gods don't
leave evidence, gifts under trees.


*Antarctica*

I handed in an eighteen-page
project on Antarctica.
What I remember is that

polar bears don't eat penguins
and it's got nothing
to do with wrappers.

Chloe handed in one hundred
and twenty pages.
What she remembers is a letter.

*Pythagoras*

Maths exams leave us
with images of window cleaners

setting up their ladders
with scientific calculators.

*History*

*Herodotus tells ~~how you~~*
*how Xerxes' messenger*
*threatened their arrows*
*would block out the sun.*

'Just draw a line through
your mistake with
a pencil. You don't need
to black it out of existence.'

I should've listened.

*PSHE*

She talks to her friends.
Or they talk.
She mostly listens,
laughs behind her hand.

I turn back to the
page in front of me.
*What do I want to
do with my life?*


*Pigment*

Primarily
she taught me
how to mix, *ahem*,
flesh-coloured

paint. White
and red,
some yellow
and those dabs

of blue that
build the tone,
touch
by spare touch.

*Skies*

Slumped in front of a canvas,
another depiction of the world fallen flat,

advice tumbled over my shoulder,
down into my lap. *You know,*

*skies should fade as they near the ground.*
A twelve-year struggle over.

# Reality

But the world is fake. Birds are animatronic.
Trees are papier mâché. Clouds are painted
on the sky; their metal linings rust and tarnish.
The river is a woven fabric and fish
are simply tears. Money's just an idea
and everything's for sale. The sun and moon
can be switched off, and clocks keep anything
but time, and what we witness in the mirror
is anything but ourselves; what we see in photos
less. Beauty is designed and dreams
are drawn by those who cannot sleep.
God is just a man and his people made of paper:
they blow away. The houses and the theatres
and churches will collapse in on themselves
like cards. Reach out, touch them. The fire
which consumes us is only an illusion.
The streets we live on are just lines
sketched onto maps which lead back to themselves.
Nothing we're taught at school is knowledge
and none of it worth knowing. We speak as though
we're on TV and our ratings are falling.
The speaker in these poems isn't me.

## As It Was

The clearing
where you stand on tiptoes
you never stood

The trees you flick between
mark a trail
we never followed

The wind
tugs at that purple dress
you never wore

The smile
you run back to me to give
you never smiled

That secret
you're still whispering
was never yours, never shared

So far we walked
and praised together and yet
we never did

# History

*'What I have written, I have written'*
*— John 19.22*

December 1$^{st}$ 1878:
the blind, all of them, met to discuss
the impracticalities of sight.

March 30$^{th}$ 1912:
four unacquainted deaf men
published near-identical essays deconstructing
the assumed importance of sound.

January 21$^{st}$ 1926:
an assembly of mutes devised a sign
for *the intrinsic paper-thinness of facts*.

April 3$^{rd}$ 1974:
thirteen men around a table,
all blind, deaf, dumb.
No one said a word.

# Acknowledgements

For my reworkings of Ovid (*Narcissus* and *Pygmalion*) I am particularly indebted to David Raeburn's translation, but also those by A.D. Melville, Mary Innes and Brookes More.

For *Alcibiades*, I am indebted to the translation of Plato's *Symposium* by Walter Hamilton, as well as those by Christopher Gill and Harold. N Fowler. Robert Fagles's *Odyssey* has also been indispensable. The quote from Socrates is apocryphal.

Lucretius's *The Nature of Things* I read in A.E. Stallings's translation, and Alain-Fournier's *Le Grand Meaulnes* in Robin Buss's translation.

Thank you to the magazines in which some of these poems have previously appeared: *The Rialto, And Other Poems, Ink Sweat & Tears, Material, Nutshells & Nuggets, Words in the Garden* and *Dream Catcher*.

Lightning Source UK Ltd.
Milton Keynes UK
UKHW011847200219
337630UK00005B/149/P